DETERMINISM,
INDETERMINISM, AND
LIBERTARIANISM

T0364330

DETERMINISM, INDETERMINISM, AND LIBERTARIANISM

BY

C. D. BROAD

*Litt.D., Knightbridge Professor of Moral Philosophy
in the University of Cambridge*

AN INAUGURAL LECTURE

CAMBRIDGE

AT THE UNIVERSITY PRESS

1934

CAMBRIDGE
UNIVERSITY PRESS

University Printing House, Cambridge CB2 8BS, United Kingdom

Cambridge University Press is part of the University of Cambridge.

It furthers the University's mission by disseminating knowledge in the pursuit of education, learning and research at the highest international levels of excellence.

www.cambridge.org
Information on this title: www.cambridge.org/9781316612767

© Cambridge University Press 1934

First published 1934
First paperback edition 2016

A catalogue record for this publication is available from the British Library

ISBN 978-1-316-61276-7 Paperback

DETERMINISM, INDETERMINISM, AND LIBERTARIANISM

1. THE IMPLICATIONS OF OBLIGABILITY. We often make retrospective judgments about the past actions of ourselves or other people which take the form: "You ought not to have done the action X, which you in fact did; you ought instead to have done the action Y, which in fact you did not". If I make such a judgment about a person, and he wants to refute it, he can take two different lines of argument. (i) He may say: "I could have done Y instead of X, but you are mistaken in thinking that Y was the action that I ought to have done. In point of fact, X, the action that I did, was the one that I ought to have done. If I had done Y, I should have done what I ought not to have done". (ii) He may say: "I could not help doing X", or he may say: "Though I need not have done X, I could not possibly have done Y".

If the accused person makes an answer of the first kind, he is admitting that the alternatives "ought" and "ought not" apply to the actions X and Y, but he is objecting to my applying "ought" to Y and "ought not" to X. He is saying that "ought" applies to X, and "ought not" to Y. It is as if two people, who agree that X and Y are each either black or white, should differ because one holds that X is black and Y white, whilst the other holds that X is white and Y black. If the accused person makes an answer of the second kind, he is denying the applicability of the alternatives "ought" and "ought not". If he says: "I could not help doing X", he assumes that his critic will admit that neither "ought" nor "ought not" has any application to an action which the agent could not help doing. If he says: "Though I need not have done X, yet I could not possibly have done Y", he assumes that his critic will admit that neither "ought" nor "ought not" has any application to an action which the agent could not have done. It is as if one person should say that X is black and Y is white, and the other should answer that at least one of them is un-extended and therefore incapable of being either black or white.

1·1. OBLIGABILITY ENTAILS SUBSTITUTABILITY. Now we are concerned here only with the second kind of answer. The essential point to notice is that it is universally admitted to be a *relevant* answer. We all admit that there is some sense or other of "could" in which "ought" and "ought not" entail "could". We will now try to get clear about the connexion between these two notions.

Judgments of obligation about past actions may be divided into two classes, viz., (1) judgments about actions which were actually done, and (2) judgments about conceivable actions which were not done. Each divides into two sub-classes, and so we get the following four-fold division. (1·1) "You did X, and X was the action that you ought to have done". (1·2) "You did X, and X was an action that you ought not to have done". (2·1) "You did not do X, and X was the action that you ought to have done". And (2·2) "You did not do X, and X was an action that you ought not to have done". Now both judgments of the first class entail that you could have helped doing the action which you in fact did. If the action that you did can be said to be one that you ought to have done, or if it can be said to be one that you ought not to have done, it must be one that you *need not* have done. And, since you actually did it, it is obviously one that you *could have* done. Both judgments of the second class entail that you could have done an action which you did not in fact do. If a conceivable action which you did not do can be said to be one which you ought to have done, or if it can be said to be one that you ought not to have done, it must be one that you *could have* done. And, since you actually failed to do it, it is obviously one that you *need not* have done.

It is worth while to notice that the common phrases: "You ought to have done so and so" and "You ought not to have done so and so" are generally equivalent to our judgments (2·1) and (1·2) respectively. The former is

(4)

generally used to mean: "You did not do so and so, and that was an action which you ought to have done". The latter is generally used to mean: "You did so and so, and that was an action which you ought not to have done". But we often need to express what is expressed by our judgments (1·1) and (2·2). We often want to say that a person did what he ought on a certain occasion, and we often want to say that a person avoided doing something which he ought not to have done on a certain occasion. For this is exactly the state of affairs which exists when a person has in fact done an unpleasant duty in face of a strong temptation to shirk it by lying.

Now the importance of this connexion between "ought" and "ought not", on the one hand, and "could", on the other, is very great. People constantly make judgments of obligation of the four kinds which we have distinguished, and such judgments have constantly been made throughout the whole course of human history. Every single one of these judgments has been false unless there have been cases in which actions which *were* done could have been left undone and actions which *were not* done could have been done. And these judgments would all have been false in principle, and not merely in detail. They would have been false, not in the sense that they asserted "ought" where they should have asserted "ought not", or *vice versa*. They would be false in the sense that nothing in the world has ever had that determinable characteristic of which "ought to be done" and "ought not to be done" are the determinate specifications. They would be false in the sense in which all judgments which predicated redness, blueness, etc., of any object would be false in a world which contained no objects except minds and noises.

It will be convenient to call an action "obligable" if and only if it is an action of which "ought to be done" or "ought not to be done" can be predicated. It will be convenient to call an action "substitutable" if, either it was done but could have been left undone, or it was left undone but could have been done. We may then sum up the situation by saying that an action is obligable if and only if it is, in a certain sense, substitutable; that, unless all judgments of obligation are false in principle, there are obligable actions; and therefore, unless all judgments of obligation are false in principle, there are actions which are, in this sense, substitutable.

1·2. VARIOUS SENSES OF "SUBSTITUTABLE". This is one aspect of the case. The other aspect is the following. There are several senses of "could" in which nearly everyone would admit that some actions which were done could have been left undone, and some actions which were left undone could have been done. There are thus several senses of "substitutable" in which it would commonly be admitted that some actions are substitutable. But, although an action which was *not* substitutable in these senses would *not* be obligable, it seems doubtful whether an action which was substitutable *only* in these senses *would be* obligable. It seems doubtful whether an action would be obligable unless it were substitutable in some further sense.

At this stage two difficulties arise. (i) It is extremely difficult to grasp and to express clearly this further sense of "substitutable", i.e., this further sense of "could" in which an action that was done could have been left undone or an action which was not done could have been done. Many people would say that they can attach no meaning to "substitutable" except those meanings in which it is insufficient to make an action obligable. (ii) Even if this other meaning of "substitutable" can be grasped and clearly expressed, many people would say that no action is substitutable in this sense. They would claim to see that no action which has been done could have been left undone, and that no action which was not done could have been done, in that sense of "could" which is required if an action is to be obligable.

Now anyone who holds these views is in a very awkward position. On the one hand, it is not easy to believe that every judgment of obligation is false, in the sense in which every judgment ascribing colour to an object would be false in a world containing only minds and noises. On the other hand, it is highly depressing to have to admit that there is a sense of "could" which you can neither grasp nor clearly express. And it is equally unsatisfactory to have to believe that some actions *are* substitutable in a sense in which it seems to you self-evident that no action *could be* substitutable.

There are two problems to be tackled at this point. (i) To try to discover and state the sense of "substitutable" in which being substitutable is the necessary and sufficient condition of being obligable. And (ii), if we can do this, to consider whether any action could be substitutable in this sense.

1·21. VOLUNTARY SUBSTITUTABILITY. Let us begin by considering an action which has actually been performed. In some cases we should say that the agent "could not have helped" performing it. We should certainly say this if we had reason to believe that the very same act would have been performed by the agent in these circumstances even though he had willed that it should not take place. It is obvious that there are actions which are "inevitable", in this sense, since there are actions which take place although the agent is trying his hardest to prevent them. Cf., e.g., the case of a conspirator taken with an uncontrollable fit of sneezing.

Next consider a conceivable action which was not in fact performed. In some cases we should say that the agent "could not possibly" have performed it. We should certainly say this if the act would not have taken place in these circumstances no matter how strongly the agent had willed it. It is obvious that there are conceivable acts which are "impossible" in this sense, since there are cases where such an act fails to take place although the agent is trying his hardest to bring it about. Cf., e.g., the case of a man who is bound and gagged, and tries vainly to give warning to a friend.

We will call acts of these two kinds "not voluntarily substitutable". It is plain that an act which is not voluntarily substitutable is not obligable. No one would say that the conspirator ought not to have sneezed, or that the bound and gagged man ought to have warned his friend. At most we may be able to say that they ought or ought not to have done certain things in the past which are relevant to their present situation. Perhaps the conspirator ought to have sprayed his nose with cocaine before hiding behind the presumably dusty arras, and perhaps the victim ought not to have let himself be lured into the house in which he was gagged and bound. But these are previous questions.

We see then that to be voluntarily substitutable is a *necessary* condition for an action to be obligable. But is it a *sufficient* condition? Suppose I performed the action A on a certain occasion. Suppose that I should not have done A then if I had willed with a certain degree of force and persistence not to do it. Since I did A, it is certain that I *did not* will with this degree of force and persistence to avoid doing it. Now suppose that at the time I *could not* have willed with this degree of force and persistence to avoid doing A. Should we be prepared to say that I ought not to have done A?

Now take another case. Suppose that on a certain occasion I failed to do a certain conceivable action B. Suppose that I should have done B if I had willed with a certain degree of force and persistence to do it. Since I did not do *B*, it is certain that I *did not* will with this degree of force and persistence to do it. Now suppose that at the time I *could not* have willed with this degree of force and persistence to do *B*. Should we be prepared to say that I ought to have done *B*? It seems to me almost certain that, under the supposed conditions, we should not be prepared to say either that I ought not to have done *A* or that I ought to have done *B*.

Consider, e.g., the case of a man who gradually becomes addicted to some drug like morphine, and eventually becomes a slave to it. At the early stages we should probably hold that he could have willed with enough force and persistence to ensure that the temptation would be resisted. At the latest stages we should probably hold that he could not have done so. Now at every stage, from the earliest to the latest, the hypothetical proposition would be true: "If he had willed with a certain degree of force and persistence to avoid taking morphine, he would have avoided taking it". Yet we should say at the earlier stages that he ought to have resisted, whilst, at the final stages, we should be inclined to say that "ought" and "ought not" have ceased to apply.

1·211. PRIMARY AND SECONDARY SUBSTITUTABILITY. An action which was in fact done, but would not have been done if there had been a strong and persistent enough desire in the agent not to do it, will be called "primarily avoidable". Suppose, in addition, that there could have been in the agent at the time a desire of sufficient strength and persistence to prevent the action being done. Then the action might be called "secondarily avoidable". If this latter condition is not fulfilled, we shall say that the action was "primarily avoidable, but secondarily inevitable". Similarly, an action which was not in fact done, but would have been done if there had been in the agent a strong and persistent enough desire to do it, will be called "primarily possible". Suppose, in addition, that there could have been in the agent at the time a desire of sufficient strength and persistence to ensure the action being done. Then the action may be called "secondarily possible". If this latter condition is not fulfilled, we shall say that the action is "primarily possible, but secondarily impossible". An action will be called "primarily substitutable" if it is either primarily avoidable or primarily possible. It will be secondarily substitutable if it is either secondarily avoidable or secondarily possible. In order that an action may be obligable it is not enough that it should be primarily substitutable, it must be at least secondarily substitutable.

We are thus led on from the notion of voluntarily substitutable *actions* to that of substitutable *volitions*. Suppose that, on a certain occasion and in a certain situation, a certain agent willed a certain alternative with a certain degree of force and persistence. We may say that the volition was substitutable if the same agent, on the same occasion and in the same circumstances, could instead have willed a different alternative or could have willed the same alternative with a different degree of force and persistence. Now there is one sense of "could" in which it might plausibly be suggested that many volitions are substitutable. It seems very likely that there are many occasions on which I *should* have willed otherwise than I did, *if* on previous occasions I had willed otherwise than I did. So it seems likely that many volitions have been voluntarily substitutable.

It is necessary to be careful at this point, or we may be inadvertently granting more than we are really prepared to admit. Obviously it is often true that, if I had willed otherwise than I did on certain earlier occasions, I should never have got into the position in which I afterwards made a certain decision. If, e.g., Julius Caesar had decided earlier in his career not to accept the command in Gaul, he would never have been in the situation in which he decided to cross the Rubicon. This, however, does not make his decision to cross the Rubicon substitutable. For a volition is substitutable only if a different volition could have occurred in the agent in the *same* situation. Again, it is often true that, if I had willed otherwise than I did on certain earlier occasions, my state of knowledge and belief would have been different on certain later occasions from what it in fact was. In that case I should have thought, on these later occasions, of certain alternatives which I did not and could not think of in my actual state of knowledge and belief. Suppose, e.g., that a lawyer has to decide what to do when a friend has met with an accident. If this man had decided years before to study medicine instead of law, it is quite likely that he would now think of, and perhaps choose, an alternative which his lack of medical knowledge prevents him from contemplating. This, however, does not make the lawyer's volition in the actual situation substitutable. For, although the external part of the total situation might have been the same whether he had previously decided to study medicine or to study law, the internal part of the total situation would have been different if he had decided to study medicine, instead of deciding, as he did, to study law. He would have become an agent with different cognitive powers and dispositions from those which he in fact has. No one would think of saying that the lawyer ought to have done a certain action, which he did not and could not contemplate, merely because he would have contemplated it and would have decided to do it if he had decided years before to become a doctor instead of becoming a lawyer.

Having cleared these irrelevances away, we can now come to the real point. A man's present conative-emotional dispositions, and what we may call his "power of intense and persistent willing", are in part dependent on his earlier volitions. If a person has repeatedly chosen the easier of the alternatives open to him, it becomes increasingly difficult for him to choose and to persist in pursuing the harder of two alternatives. If he has formed a habit of turning his attention away from certain kinds of fact, it will become increasingly difficult for him to attend fairly to alternatives which involve facts of these kinds. This is one aspect of the case. Another, and equally important, aspect is the following. If a man reflects on his own past decisions, he may see that he has a tendency to ignore or to dwell upon certain kinds of fact, and that this had led him to make unfair or unwise decisions on many occasions. He may decide that, in future, he will make a special effort to give due, and not more than due, weight to those considerations which he has a tendency to ignore or to dwell upon. And this decision may make a difference to his future decisions. On the other hand, he may see that certain alternatives have a specially strong attraction for him, and he may find that, if he pays more than a fleeting attention to them, he will be rushed into choosing them, and will afterwards regret it. He may decide that, in future, he will think as little as possible about such alternatives. And this decision may make a profound difference to his future decisions.

We can now state the position in general terms. Suppose that, if the agent had willed differently on earlier occasions, his conative-emotional dispositions and his knowledge of his own nature would have been so modified that he would now have willed differently in the actual external situation and in his actual state of knowledge and belief about the alternatives open to him. Then we can say that his actual volition in the present situation was "voluntarily avoidable", and that a volition of a different kind or of a different degree of force and persistence was "voluntarily possible". An action which took place was secondarily avoidable if the following two conditions are fulfilled. (i) That this action would not have been done if the agent had willed with a certain degree of force and persistence to avoid it. (ii) That, if he had willed differently in the past, his conative-emotional dispositions and his knowledge of his own nature would have been such, at the time when he did the action, that he would have willed to avoid it with enough force and persistence to prevent him doing it. In a precisely similar way we could define the statement that a certain conceivable action, which was not done, was secondarily possible. And we can thus define the statement that an action is secondarily substitutable.

Can we say that an action is obligable if it is secondarily substitutable, in the sense just defined, though it is not obligable if it is only primarily substitutable? It seems to me that the same difficulty which we noticed before reappears here. Suppose that the agent could not have willed otherwise than he did in the remoter past. It is surely irrelevant to say that, *if* he had done so, his conative dispositions *would* have been different at a later stage from what they in fact were then, and that he *would* have willed otherwise than he then did. One might, of course, try to deal with this situation by referring back to still earlier volitions. One might talk of actions which are not only primarily, or only secondarily, but are tertiarily substitutable. But it is quite clear that this is useless. If neither primary nor secondary substitutability, in the sense defined, suffice to make an action obligable, no higher order of substitutability, in this sense, will suffice. The further moves are of exactly the same nature as the second move. And so, if the second move does not get us out of the difficulty, none of the further moves will do so.

1·22. CATEGORICAL SUBSTITUTABILITY. The kind of substitutability which we have so far considered may be called "conditional substitutability". For at every stage we have defined "could" to mean "would have been, if certain conditions had been fulfilled which were not". Now I have concluded that merely conditional substitutability, of however high an order, is not a sufficient condition for obligability. If an action is to be obligable, it must be *categorically* substitutable. We must be able to say of an action, which was done, that it could have been avoided, in some sense of "could" which is not definable in terms of "would have, if". And we must be able to say of a conceivable action, which was not done, that it could have been done, in some sense of "could" which is not definable in terms of "would have, if". Unless there are some actions of which such things can truly be said, there are no actions which are obligable. We must therefore consider whether any clear meaning can be attached to the phrase "categorically substitutable", i.e., whether "could" has any clear meaning except "would have, if". And, if we can find such a meaning, we must enquire whether any actions are categorically substitutable.

1·221. VARIOUS SENSES OF "OBLIGABLE". Before tackling these questions I must point out that the words "ought" and "ought not" are used in several different senses. In some of these senses obligability does not entail categorical substitutability.

(i) There is a sense of "ought" in which we apply it even to inanimate objects. It would be quite proper to say: "A car ought to be able to get from London to Cambridge in less than three hours", or: "A fountain-pen ought not to be constantly making blots". We mean by this simply that a car which did take more than three hours would be a poor specimen of car, or would be in a bad state of repair. And similar remarks apply to the statement about the fountain-pen. We are comparing the behaviour of a certain car or fountain-pen with the average standard of achievement of cars or fountain-pens. We are not suggesting that *this* car or *this* pen, in its present state of repair, unconditionally could go faster or avoid making blots. Sometimes when we make such judgments we are comparing an individual's achievements, not with those of the *average* member, but with those of an *ideally perfect* member, of a certain class to which it belongs. We will call "ought", in this sense, "the comparative ought". And we can then distinguish "the average-comparative ought" and "the ideal-comparative ought".

(ii) Plainly "ought" and "ought not" can be, and often are, used in this sense of human actions. But, in the case of human actions, there is a further development. Since a human being has the power of cognition, in general, and of reflexive cognition, in particular, he can have an idea of an average or an ideal man. He can compare his own achievements with those of the average, or the ideal, man, as conceived by him. And he will have a more or less strong and persistent desire to approximate to the ideal and not to fall below the average. Now it is part of the notion of an ideal man that he is a being who would have a high ideal of human nature and would desire strongly and persistently to approximate to his ideal. Obviously it is no part of the notion of an ideal horse or an ideal car that it is a being which would have a high ideal of horses or cars and a strong and persistent desire to live up to this. When we say that a man ought not to cheat at cards we often mean to assert two things. (*a*) That the average decent man does not do this, and that anyone who does falls in this respect below the average. And (*b*) that a man who does this either has a very low ideal of human nature or a very weak and unstable desire to approximate to the ideal which he has. So that, in this further respect, he falls below the average.

Now neither of these judgments implies that a particular person, who cheated on a particular occasion, categorically could have avoided cheating then; or that he categorically could have had a higher ideal of human nature; or that he categorically could have willed more strongly and persistently to live up to the ideal which he had. For an action to be obligable, in this sense, it is plainly enough that it should be secondarily substitutable, in the sense already defined.

1·2211. THE CATEGORICAL OUGHT. Some philosophers of great eminence, e.g., Spinoza, have held that the sense of "ought" which I have just discussed is the only sense of it. Plainly it is a very important sense, and it is one in which "ought" and "ought not" can be applied only to the actions of intelligent beings with powers of reflexive cognition, emotion, and conation. I think that a clear-headed Determinist should hold either that this is the only sense; or that, if there is another sense, in which obligability entails *categorical* substitutability, it has no application.

Most people, however, would say that, although we often do use "ought" and "ought not" in this sense, we quite often use them in another sense, and that in this other sense they entail categorical substitutability. I am inclined to think that this is true. When I judge that I ought not to have done something which I in fact did, I do not as a rule seem to be judging merely that a person with higher ideals, or with a stronger and more persistent desire to live up to his ideals, would not have done what I did. Even when this is part of what I mean, there seems to be something more implied in my judgment, viz., that I *could* have had higher ideals or *could* have willed more strongly and persistently to live up to my ideals, where "could" does not mean just "would have, if". Let us call this sense of "ought" the "categorical ought". It seems to me then that we must distinguish between an action being obligable in the comparative sense and being obligable in the categorical sense; and that, if any action were categorically obligable, it would have to be categorically substitutable.

1·222. ANALYSIS OF CATEGORICAL SUBSTITUTABILITY. We can now proceed to discuss the notion of categorical substitutability. It seems to me to involve a negative and a positive condition. I think that the negative condition can be clearly formulated, and that there is no insuperable difficulty in admitting that it may sometimes be fulfilled. The ultimate difficulty is to give any intelligible account of the positive condition. I will now explain and illustrate these statements.

Suppose that, on a certain occasion, I willed a certain alternative with a certain degree of force and persistence, and that, in consequence of this volition, I did a certain voluntary action which I should not have done unless I had willed this alternative with this degree of intensity and persistence. To say that I categorically could have avoided doing this action

(26)

implies at least that the following negative condition is fulfilled. It implies that the process of my willing this alternative with this degree of force and persistence was not completely determined by the nomic, the occurrent, the dispositional, and the background conditions which existed immediately before and during this process of willing. In order to see exactly what this means it will be best to contrast it with a case in which we believe that a process is completely determined by such conditions.

Suppose that two billiard-balls are moving on a table, that they collide at a certain moment, and that they go on moving in modified directions with modified velocities in consequence of the impact. Let us take as universal premises the general laws of motion and of elastic impact. We will call these "nomic premises". Let us take as singular premises the following propositions. (i) That each ball was moving in such and such a direction with such and such a velocity at the moment of impact. We will call these "occurrent premises". (ii) That the masses and coefficients of elasticity of the balls were such and such. We will call these "dispositional premises". (iii) That the table was smooth and level before, at, and after the moment of impact. We will call this a "background premise". Lastly, let us take the proposition that the balls are moving, directly after the impact, in such and such directions with such and such velocities. Then this last proposition is a *logical consequence* of the conjunction of the nomic, the occurrent, the dispositional, and the background premises. That is to say, the combination of these premises with the denial of the last proposition would be *logically inconsistent*. It is so in exactly the sense in which the combination of the premises of a valid syllogism with the denial of its conclusion would be so.

1·2221. THE NEGATIVE CONDITION. We can now work towards a definition of the statement that a certain event *e* was completely determined in respect of a certain characteristic. When we have defined this statement it will be easy to define the statement that a certain event was not completely determined in respect of a certain characteristic. I will begin with a concrete example, and will then generalise the result into a definition.

Suppose that a certain flash happened at a certain place and date. This will be a manifestation of a certain determinable characteristic, viz., colour, in a certain perfectly determinate form. It may, e.g., be a red flash of a certain perfectly determinate shade, intensity, and saturation. We may call shade, intensity, and saturation the three "dimensions" of colour, and we shall therefore symbolise the determinable characteristic colour by a three-suffix symbol C_{123}. When we want to symbolise a certain perfectly determinate value of this we shall use the symbol C_{123}^{abc}. This means that the shade has the determinate value a, that the intensity has the determinate value b, and that the saturation has the determinate value c. Each *index* indicates the determinate value which the dimension indicated by the corresponding *suffix* has in the given instance.

Now the statement that this flash was completely determined in respect of colour has the following meaning. It means that there is a set of true nomic, occurrent, dispositional, and background propositions which together entail the proposition that a manifestation of colour, of the precise shade, intensity, and saturation which this flash manifested, happened at the place and time at which this flash happened. To say that this flash was *not* completely determined in respect of colour means that there is *no* set of true nomic, occurrent, dispositional, and background propositions which together entail the proposition that a manifestation of colour, of the precise shade, intensity, and saturation which this flash manifested, happened at the place and time at which this flash happened.

There are two remarks to be made at this point. (i) It seems to me that the second statement is perfectly *intelligible*, even if no such statement be ever true. (ii) It is a purely *ontological* statement, and not in any way a statement about the limitations of our knowledge. Either there is such a set of true propositions, or there is not. There may be such a set, even if no one knows that there is; and there may be no such set, even if everyone believes that there is.

We can now give a general definition. The statement that a certain event e was completely determined in respect of a certain determinable characteristic C_{123} is equivalent to the conjunction of the following two propositions. (i) The event e was a manifestation of C_{123} in a certain perfectly determinate form C_{123}^{abc} at a certain place and date. (ii) There is a set of true nomic, occurrent, dispositional, and background propositions which together entail that a manifestation of C_{123} in the form C_{123}^{abc} happened at the place and date at which e happened. The statement that e was *not* completely determined in respect of C_{123} is equivalent to the conjoint assertion of (i) and denial of (ii).

The next point to notice is that an event might be partly determined and partly undetermined in respect of a certain characteristic. As before, I will begin with a concrete example. Our flash might be completely determined in respect of shade and saturation, but not in respect of intensity. This would be equivalent to the conjunction of the following two statements. (i) That there is a set of true propositions, of the kind already mentioned, which together entail that a flash, of precisely the shade and saturation which this flash had, happened at the place and date at which this flash happened. (ii) There is no such set of true propositions which together entail that a flash, of precisely the intensity which this flash had, happened at the time and place at which this flash happened. We thus get the notion of "orders of indetermination" in respect of a given characteristic. If an event is undetermined in respect of one and only one dimension of a certain determinable characteristic, we say that it has "indetermination of the first order" in respect of this characteristic. If it is undetermined in respect of two and only two dimensions of a certain determinable characteristic, we say that it has "indetermination of the second order" in respect of this characteristic. And so on.

It is obvious that there is another possibility to be considered, which I will call "range of indetermination in respect of a given dimension of a given characteristic". Suppose that our flash is undetermined in respect of the intensity of its colour. There may be a set of true propositions, of the kind mentioned, which together entail that a flash, whose intensity falls within certain limits, happened at the time and place at which this flash happened. This range of indetermination may be wide or narrow. Complete determination in respect of a given dimension of a given characteristic is the limiting case where the range of indetermination shuts up to zero about the actual value of this dimension for this event. Thus the "extent of indetermination" of an event with respect to a given characteristic depends in general upon two factors, viz., (i) its order of indetermination with respect to the dimensions of this characteristic, and (ii) its range of indetermination with respect to those dimensions for which it is not completely determined.

We can now define the statement that a certain event e was completely determined. It means that e has zero range of indetermination for every dimension of every determinable characteristic of which it is a manifestation. The statement that a certain event e was *not* completely determined can now be defined. It means that *e* had a finite range of indetermination for at least one dimension of at least one of the characteristics of which it was a manifestation.

And now at last we can define "Determinism" and "Indeterminism". Determinism is the doctrine that *every* event is completely determined, in the sense just defined. Indeterminism is the doctrine that some, and it may be all, events are not completely determined, in the sense defined. Both doctrines are, *prima facie*, intelligible, when defined as I have defined them.

There is one other point to be noticed. An event might be completely determined, and yet it might have a "causal ancestor" which was not completely determined. If Y is the total cause of Z, and X is the total cause of Y, I call both Y and X "causal ancestors" of Z. Similarly, if W were the total cause of X, I should call Y, X, and W "causal ancestors" of Z. And so on. If at any stage in such a series there is a term, e.g., W, which contains a cause-factor that is not completely determined, the series will stop there, just as the series of human ancestors stops with Adam. Such a term may be called the "causal progenitor" of such a series. If Determinism be true, every event has causal ancestors, and therefore there are no causal progenitors. If Indeterminism be true, there are causal progenitors in the history of the world.

We can now state the negative condition which must be fulfilled if an action is to be categorically substitutable. Suppose that, at a certain time, an agent deliberated between two alternatives, A and B, and that he actually did A and not B. Suppose that the following conditions are fulfilled. (i) The doing of A by this agent at this moment was completely determined. (ii) The total cause of A being done contained as cause-factors a desire of a certain strength and persistence for A and a desire of a certain strength and persistence for B. (iii) These two desires were not completely determined in respect of strength and persistence. (iv) The range of indetermination was wide enough to include in it, as possible values, so strong and persistent a desire for B or so weak and fleeting a desire for A as would have determined the doing of B instead of the doing of A. Conditions (iii) and (iv) are the negative conditions which must be fulfilled if B is to be categorically substitutable for A. They amount to the following statement. It is consistent with (a) the laws of nature, including those of psychology, (b) the facts about the agent's dispositions and the dispositions of any other agent in the world at the moment of acting, (c) the facts about what was happening within and without the agent at that moment, and (d) the facts about the general background conditions at that moment, that the strength and persistence of the desires mentioned in (ii) should have any value that falls within the range mentioned in (iv).

Before we go further there is one point to be mentioned. Strictly speaking, what I have just stated are the negative conditions for *primary* categorical substitutability. For I have supposed the incomplete determination to occur at the *first* stage backwards, viz., in one of the cause-factors in the total cause of the action A. It would be quite easy to define, in a similar way, the negative conditions for secondary, or tertiary, or any other order of categorical substitutability. All that is needed is that, at *some* stage in the causal ancestry of *A*, there shall be a total cause which contains as factors desires of the agent answering to the conditions which I have stated. That is to say, all that is necessary is that *A* shall have a causal ancestor which is a causal progenitor, containing as a factor an incompletely determined desire of the agent's.

We come now to the final question. Supposing that this negative condition were fulfilled, would this *suffice* to make an action categorically obligable? It seems to me plain that it would not. Unless some further and positive condition were fulfilled, all that one could say would be the following: "The desire to do *A* happened to be present in me with such strength and persistence, as compared with the desire to do *B*, that I did *A* and avoided *B*. The desire to do *B* might have happened to be present in me with such strength and persistence, as compared with the desire to do *A*, that I should have done *B* and avoided *A*". Now, if this is all, the fact that I did A and not B is, in the strictest sense, an *accident*, lucky or unlucky as the case may be. It may be welcomed or it may be deplored, but neither I nor anything else in the universe can properly be praised or blamed for it. It begins to look as if the categorical ought may be inapplicable, though for different reasons, both on the hypothesis that voluntary actions have causal progenitors and on the hypothesis that none of their causal ancestors are causal progenitors.

1·2222. THE POSITIVE CONDITION. Let us now try to discover the positive conditions of categorical obligability. I think that we should naturally tend to answer the sort of objection which I have just raised in the following way. We should say: "I deliberately identified myself with my desire to do A, or I deliberately threw my weight on the side of that desire. I might instead have made no particular effort in one direction or the other; or I might have identified myself with, and thrown my weight on the side of, my desire to do B. So my desire to do A did not just happen to be present with the requisite strength and persistence, as compared with my desire to do B. It had this degree of strength and persistence because, and only because, I *reinforced* it by a deliberate effort, which I need not have made at all and which I could have made in favour of my desire to do B". Another way of expressing the same thing would be this: "I forced myself to do A; but I need not have done so, and, if I had not done so, I should have done B". Or again: "I might have forced myself to do B; but I did not, and so I did A".

It is quite plain that these phrases express a genuine positive experience with which we are all perfectly familiar. They are all, of course, metaphorical. It will be noticed that they all attempt to describe the generic fact by metaphors drawn from specific instances of it, e.g., deliberately pressing down one scale of a balance, deliberately joining one side in a tug-of-war, deliberately thrusting a body in a certain direction against obstacles, and so on. In this respect they may be compared with attempts to describe the generic facts about time and change by metaphors drawn from specific instances, such as flowing streams, moving spots of light, and so on. The only use of such metaphors is to direct attention to the sort of fact which one wants one's hearers to contemplate. They give no help towards analysing or comprehending this fact. A metaphor helps us to understand a fact only when it brings out an analogy with a fact of a *different* kind, which we already understand. When a generic fact can be described only by metaphors drawn from specific instances of itself it is a sign that the fact is unique and peculiar, like the fact of temporal succession and the change of events from futurity, through presentness, to pastness.

Granted that there is this unique and peculiar factor of deliberate effort or reinforcement, how far does the recognition of it help us in our present problem? So far as I can see, it merely takes the problem one step further back. My doing of A is completely determined by a total cause which contains as factors my desire to do A and my desire to do B, each of which has a certain determinate strength and persistence. The preponderance of my desire to do *A* over my desire to do *B*, in respect of strength and persistence, is completely determined by a total cause which contains as a factor my putting forth a certain amount of effort to reinforce my desire for *A*. This effort-factor is not completely determined. It is logically consistent with all the nomic, occurrent, dispositional, and background facts that no effort should have been made, or that it should have been directed towards reinforcing the desire for *B* instead of the desire for *A*, or that it should have been put forth more or less strongly than it actually was in favour of the desire for *A*. Surely then we can say no more than that it just happened to occur with a certain degree of intensity in favour of the desire for *A*.

I think that the safest course at this stage for those who maintain that some actions are categorically obligable would be the following. They should admit quite frankly what I have just stated, and should then say: "However paradoxical it may seem, we do regard ourselves and other people as morally responsible for accidents of this unique kind, and we do not regard them as morally responsible, in the categorical sense, for anything but such accidents and those consequences of them which would have been different if the accidents had happened differently. Only such accidents, and their causal descendants in the way of volition and action, are categorically obligable". If anyone should take up this position, I should not know how to refute him, though I should be strongly inclined to think him mistaken.

This is not, however, the position which persons who hold that some actions are categorically obligable generally do take at this point. I do not find that they ever state quite clearly what they think they believe, and I suspect that this is because, if it were clearly stated, it would be seen to be impossible. I shall therefore try to state clearly what I think such people want to believe, and shall try to show that it is impossible. I suspect that they would quarrel with my statement that, on their view, the fact that one puts forth such and such an effort in support of a certain desire is, in the strictest sense, an accident. They would like to say that the putting forth of a certain amount of effort in a certain direction at a certain time *is* completely determined, but is determined in a unique and peculiar way. It is literally determined *by the agent or self*, considered as a substance or continuant, and not by a total cause which contains as factors *events in* and *dispositions of* the agent. If this could be maintained, our puttings-forth of effort would be completely determined, but their causes would neither be events nor contain events as cause-factors. Certain series of events would then originate from causal progenitors which are continuants and not events. Since the first event in such a series would be completely determined, it would not be an accident. And, since the total cause of such an event would not be an event and would not contain an event as a cause-factor, the two alternatives "completely determined" and "partially undetermined" would both be inapplicable to it. For these alternatives apply only to events.

I am fairly sure that this is the kind of proposition which people who profess to believe in Free Will want to believe. I have, of course, stated it with a regrettable crudity, of which they would be incapable. Now it seems to me clear that such a view is impossible. The putting-forth of an effort of a certain intensity, in a certain direction, at a certain moment, for a certain duration, is quite clearly an event or process, however unique and peculiar it may be in other respects. It is therefore subject to any conditions which self-evidently apply to every event, as such. Now it is surely quite evident that, if the beginning of a certain process at a certain time is determined at all, its total cause *must* contain as an essential factor another event or process which *enters into* the moment from which the determined event or process *issues*. I see no *prima facie* objection to there being events that are not completely determined. But, in so far as an event *is* determined, an essential factor in its total cause must be other *events*. How could an event possibly be determined to happen at a certain date if its total cause contained no factor to which the notion of date has any application? And how can the notion of date have any application to anything that is not an event?

Of course I am well aware that we constantly use phrases, describing causal transactions, in which a continuant is named as the cause and no event in that continuant is mentioned. Thus we say: "The stone broke the window", "The cat killed the mouse", and so on. But it is quite evident that all such phrases are elliptical. The first, e.g., expresses what would be more fully expressed by the sentence: "The coming in contact of the moving stone with the window at a certain moment caused a process of disintegration to begin in the window at that moment". Thus the fact that we use and understand such phrases casts no doubt on the general principle which I have just enunciated.

Let us call the kind of causation which I have just described and rejected "non-occurrent causation of events". We will call the ordinary kind of causation, which I had in mind when I defined "Determinism" and "Indeterminism", "occurrent causation".

Now I think we can plausibly suggest what

may have made some people think they believe that puttings-forth of effort are events which are determined by non-occurrent causation. It is quite usual to say that a man's putting-forth of effort in a certain direction on a certain occasion was determined by "Reason" or "Principle" or "Conscience" or "The Moral Law". Now these impressive names and phrases certainly do not denote events or even substances. If they denote anything, they stand for propositions or systems of pro-positions, or for those peculiar universals or systems of universals which Plato called "Ideas". If it were literally true that puttings-forth of effort are determined by such entities, we should have causation of events in time by timeless causes. But, of course, statements like "Smith's putting-forth of effort in a certain direction on a certain occasion was determined by the Moral Law" cannot be taken literally. The Moral Law, as such, has no causal efficacy. What is meant is that Smith's *belief* that a certain alternative would be in accordance with the Moral Law, and his *desire* to do what is right, were cause-factors in the total cause which determined his putting-forth of effort on the side of that alternative. Now this belief was an event, which happened when he began to reflect on the alternatives and to consider them in the light of the moral principles which he accepts and regards as relevant. And this desire was an event, which happened when his conative-emotional moral dispositions were stirred by the process of reflecting on the alternatives. Thus the use of phrases about action being "determined by the Moral Law" may have made some people think they believe that some events are determined by non-occurrent causation. But our analysis of the meaning of such phrases shows that the facts which they express give no logical support to this belief.

1·3. LIBERTARIANISM. We are now in a position to define what I will call "Libertarianism". This doctrine may be summed up in two propositions. (i) Some (and it may be all) voluntary actions have a causal ancestor which contains as a cause-factor the putting-forth of an effort which is not completely determined in direction and intensity by occurrent causation. (ii) In such cases the direction and the intensity of the effort are completely determined by non-occurrent causation, in which the self or agent, taken as a substance or continuant, is the non-occurrent total cause. Thus, Libertarianism, as defined by me, entails Indeterminism, as defined by me; but the converse does not hold.

If I am right, Libertarianism is self-evidently impossible, whilst Indeterminism is *prima facie* possible. Hence, if categorical obligability entails Libertarianism, it is certain that no action can be categorically obligable. But if categorical obligability entails only Indeterminism, it is *prima facie* possible that some actions are categorically obligable. Unfortunately, it seems almost certain that categorical obligability entails more than Indeterminism, and it seems very likely that it entails Libertarianism. It is therefore highly probable that the notion of categorical obligability is a delusive notion, which neither has nor can have any application.

www.ingramcontent.com/pod-product-compliance
Ingram Content Group UK Ltd.
Pitfield, Milton Keynes, MK11 3LW, UK
UKHW042141280225
455719UK00001B/4

9 781316 612767